Storytelling with Puppets, Props, and Playful Tales

Written by

Mary Jo Huff

 Brilliant Publications

Publishers' information

Published by: **Brilliant Publications,**
1 Church View,
Sparrow Hall Farm,
Edlesborough,
Dunstable,
Bedfordshire
LU6 2ES

Telephone: **01525 229720**
Fax: **01525 229725**
Website: **www.brilliantpublications.co.uk**
E-mail: **sales@brilliantpublications.co.uk**

Written by Mary Jo Huff.
Illustrated by Marilyn Barr.
© Monday Morning Books, Inc.
Originally published in the USA in 1998 by Monday Morning Books, Inc.
PO Box 1680, Palo Alto, CA 94302, USA

ISBN 1 897675 77 1
First published in UK in 2000.
10 9 8 7 6 5 4 3 2

Reprinted in the UK by Brilliant Publications

Contents

My personal thanks... Mary Jo Huff

To all the children whose eyes have lit up when they listened to a story, especially my grandchildren Kurt, Melanie, Matthew and Michael. To my family – Cathy, Joe, Melody, Kenny, John, and Nikki, who have always encouraged this endeavour; especially my husband Bill, who has endured the daily hardships of my organized chaos; my mum, who never knows what to expect next; and my dad, who had the real gift of the gab.

To the members of Friends of Storytelling. To my road partners, Sharon Hall and Carol Rogers, for their patient listening and their advice over the years. To my sister, Connie Elbrink, who teaches third grade and who has invited me to stop by to tell a story any time. To my puppet connection, Joyce Davis, who keeps her best friend in a basket. To my writing angels, Lucille VanWinkle and Christine Kallevig. To Maria Elena Buria, Billy's mother. To my USI connections: Dr Sheri Boyd; Barbara Plum, a wonderful lady and friend who loved children; and the teachers, parents, and children of Kinder Kountry Pre-School for the years of fun and support.

There is no better way to share life than with a group of children and a good story. To each of you who values the art of storytelling and enjoys this book I say, 'Hand down the past to the present and preserve the present for the future. Tell a story!'

Introduction

In today's modern world storytelling has become a lost art. Paper and pen, the typewriter, and now the computer have replaced the oral story sharing that was once the way to keep our cultures and heritage alive.

But things are changing. The ancient art of storytelling is being resurrected to once again play an important role within families and as part of school curricula. As an early childhood educator for 24 years and a professional storyteller for 6, I am very happy to see this new interest. And since I believe that everyone is a storyteller, I have written **Storytelling with Puppets, Props and Playful Tales** to motivate you to find the storyteller within yourself and to become creative and comfortable telling stories to young children.

Storytelling with Puppets, Props and Playful Tales is appropriate for children of all ages. Working with the ideas found in this book will help you to:
- stimulate imaginations
- develop oral communication skills
- increase auditory discrimination
- strengthen listening and pre-reading skills
- encourage creativity
- improve fine motor skills
- promote visual discrimination
- develop critical thinking skills
- strengthen sequencing skills
- encourage participation
- create a love of books, reading, and, eventually, writing.

The book is divided into three parts: **Puppets and playful tales**, **Props and playful tales**, and **Story corners and playful tales**. Storytelling techniques for the non-professional storyteller will be introduced, as well as how to make and use storytelling puppets and props and how to put together an exciting storytelling corner. Tales and chants to use with the storytelling aids are also included.

Storytelling with Puppets, Props and Playful Tales has been written with you in mind. I encourage you to take from this book storytelling ideas that are a part of my life and share them with a child. There are new and exciting story experiences waiting for you just around the corner.

Brilliant Publications
www.brilliantpublications.co.uk

Storytelling with Puppets, Props and Playful Tales
Written by Mary Jo Huff

Tips for telling stories

Discover the right story to tell:
- look for stories that are age-appropriate
- find stories that you love and believe in
- check picture books written for different age levels
- collect stories from family, friends, and community
- create your own stories.

Learn the story:
- by reading it several times
- by breaking it into a beginning, middle, and end.

Retell the story many times:
- listen to yourself telling the story
- tape-record your version
- practise telling the story to family and friends.

Speak naturally:
- use your normal speaking voice
- use sound effects, such as unusual voice and story sounds, sparingly.

Use simple, natural gestures:
- add gestures when they add to the story, but don't overuse them.

Polish the story:
- by telling it, retelling it, and retelling it.

Once you have a story ready to tell, create a story corner in which to tell it. You can set one up with the story corner props described in **Story corners and playful tales**. Then . . . BEGIN!
- make eye contact with your listeners
- introduce the story
- tell the story looking directly into your listeners' eyes
- encourage your listeners to interact with you
- enjoy and work with your audience's enthusiasm.

Developing a storytelling curriculum

To make the most of storytelling's benefits, stories need to be repeated again and again. If you use a literature-based curriculum, you'll be able to extend a story's ideas throughout the day. As you do, listen for the children retelling the story in their own special way.

The following is just a sample of how a story can be extended using **The farmer's headache**. (see pg 89–90). I encourage you to adapt these possibilities to suit your curriculum.

Story talk. Ask the children if they have ever had a headache or if someone they know has complained of a headache. Does noise bother a person with a headache? What remedies are there for a headache? Why did the farmer have a headache?

Art. The children can create stick puppets for the characters in the story and add more characters to the plot. Set out scissors, markers, sugar paper, thin card, laminated paper, glue, and ice lolly sticks. Several types of paper provide different textures for the puppets.

Cooking. Bake animal-shaped biscuits and let the children retell the story during break time.

Story corner. To help children retell the story, provide storytelling materials in a story corner. You can create a farmyard story box by cutting slits in a box top and placing stick puppets in the slits as the story unfolds. Puppets with magnets can be used on a magnetic board and story board characters can be attached to a board with Velcro™ (hook fastening) pieces. Supply the corner with plenty of books about farmers and have paper, pencils, markers, crayons, and scissors
available for children to create their own characters for storytelling.

Maths. Ask the children to count the animals annoying the farmer. Let each child choose a favourite animal and then graph the results. The children can also predict and then graph which animal made the loudest noise.

Science. Play a tape of different animal sounds and let the children identify the animals. Which animal has the loudest sound and which one has the softest? What do the animals eat? Do they live inside or outside the barn? Talk about the different sounds that children hear daily.

Brilliant Publications
www.brilliantpublications.co.uk

Storytelling with Puppets, Props and Playful Tales
Written by Mary Jo Huff

Story classifications

Storytelling with puppets and props isn't limited to just one kind of story. When you develop your storytelling curriculum, be sure to include a good variety of story types:

Fables   Short tales that have a moral and communicate a truth about life. The main characters in fables are often animals that act and think like humans.

Fairy tales Stories that often feature fairies, elves, genies, pixies, leprechauns, and other make-believe characters.

Legends   Stories that revolve around incidents that are believed to have taken place in a particular culture's history.

Folk tales   Stories that come to us from many parts of the world. These stories reflect a particular country or people's flavour and preserve cultural traditions.

Poetry   Rhyming poetry, in particular Mother Goose rhymes, is a source of excellent stories for young children.

Puppet and prop materials

Most of the materials needed for puppet and prop making are readily available and inexpensive to purchase in craft shops, supermarkets, stationers, school supply catalogues. Some of the items, such as shoe boxes, old gloves or socks and kitchen towel rolls, can be brought in from home. Construction materials for making a portable story wall will cost a bit more, but the wall will be usable for years to come.

One material which is very useful for puppet and prop-making and in the story corner is Velcro™ or hook and loop fastening products (see page 128 for suppliers). To be effective, the soft side, or loop side, must meet the rougher side, or the hook side, of another piece. Be sure when making puppets or props to use with a story board, story can, or other storytelling accessory that the hook fastening on the puppet will adhere to the loop nylon on the story board.

Self-adhesive hook fastening can be cut into small pieces that you store till needed in a plastic bag. Self-adhesive hook fastening can be stuck to art foam, poster board, laminated materials, plastic, wood, felt, and fabric. If the self-adhesive pieces do not stick well, add a drop of quick-bonding glue and press in place. When disengaging puppets or props that have been attached to a surface with hook fastening, place your thumb at the top of the item and gently pull down.

The benefits of storytelling

Puppets

Puppets are a powerful way to reach children – even a shy child will relate to a puppet. Puppets are also multisensory vehicles for storytelling, and create an art and language experience that children can understand. When you find a special puppet, and give it a personality and a home, you'll be amazed how children interact with it. Use it in your story corner and throughout your curriculum.

Props

Going beyond simply reading a story adds a great deal to the reading/ listening experience. Using props:

- creates story awareness
- helps the children to hear and feel the language
- makes each story come alive
- lets the children participate in the story and develop fine motor skills as they manipulate props and puppets
- helps the children learn to retell stories.

Story corners

Storytelling involves cooperation and interaction. This in turn promotes literacy and love of language. Encourage the children to interact during your storytelling. Also encourage parents to tell family and other stories to the children. Experience with interactive storytelling will provide a solid foundation on which to build future reading and writing skills.

Brilliant Publications
www.brilliantpublications.co.uk

Storytelling with Puppets, Props and Playful Tales
Written by Mary Jo Huff

Puppets and playful tales

Storytelling with puppets

The puppeteer

Find a story with one or two main characters – this will help since you have only two hands for holding puppets! If a story has many characters, let the children act out the smaller parts.

When you tell the story, give your puppet a special voice and character. Puppets are magical, and the audience should focus on the puppet and not the puppeteer. Find a comfort zone with your puppet and story. Children never get tired of hearing or acting out favourites, such as **Goldilocks and the three bears** and **The three little pigs**, Treat the puppets as if they were alive. REMEMBER also, that some children are not used to puppets, so proceed with caution.

Puppet voices

Once you've created a puppet, spend some time with it to learn its character. Experiment with your voice to decide what the puppet's voice should be. Using a lower pitch is easier at the beginning. Work up to a higher pitch to give yourself a three-level range: normal, high and low. Once your puppet has its own voice, you are ready to tell the story. Puppets with open mouths are more expressive.

Puppet etiquette

Puppets should never be allowed to fight. Many times children try to make puppets bite, punch, or hit each other. Give direction on how they are to use their puppets. Set limits for puppet activity and treat the puppets with respect. The children will model your behaviour.

Puppet houses

Give your puppets a place to live. Also be sure puppets have a special place to enter the story. Do not let the audience see you put on a puppet or take one off your hand.

Mascot

Giving the story corner a mascot – complete with name, voice, and personality – will help children relate to puppet storytelling. Keep the mascot puppet in a special house and bring it to life to prepare the children for circle time, story time, or as a transition tool.

Introducing the puppets

Use a soft voice at first and gradually change it as needed in the story. Move the puppet slowly. Touch the puppet gently and let it whisper in your ear or in each child's ear. Let all the children touch the puppet. Ask the children if they want the puppet to help tell a story. Provide puppets for the children to use on their own.

Box puppet

The great thing about the box puppet is that it's easy to put together. The directions are for creating a frog puppet, but different colours of paint and different types of boxes will let children produce box puppets for story characters.

Materials

2 empty jelly boxes; scissors; heavy cloth tape or duct tape; glue; brown and green paint; sponges; brush; plastic eyes; pipe cleaners or crinkled paper.

Directions

Open one end of each of the jelly boxes. Cut off three of the end flaps on each box, retaining one of the long flaps. Place the boxes side by side and tape the two flaps together with heavy tape. Paint the boxes green for a frog puppet. Then sponge-paint over the base colour different shades of brown and green. Glue on eyes and pipe cleaner or paper legs (see the illustration). Adults can work the puppet's mouth by putting a thumb in the bottom box and four fingers in the top box, but children may find it easier to put one hand in each box.

Story retelling

Let each child use a frog puppet to retell the tale **Down by the pond** (see page 38). The children can use the frogs to answer questions about the pond and take them home to use for retelling the story to their families. Keep a frog box puppet in the story corner for the children to use.

Finger puppet

Finger puppets are designed to fit on the fingers or thumb. They are small enough to fit in a shirt pocket, clear pencil case or VCR cassette box, small bag or apron pocket. They are also easy to make and store. The following directions are for a generic puppet that you and the children can decorate to fit any story.

Materials
Glove fingers
Loop nylon fabric and hook fastening
Heavy felt
Needle and thread
Upholstery fabric
Glue
Scissors
Quilt padding or cotton wool
Decorative materials

Directions
Cut out the fingers of a glove.
Glue or sew decorative items to the fingers. If the puppet is larger than a child's finger, stuff it with a small amount of padding or cotton wool. To use the finger puppet with a loop nylon fabric story board, attach a piece of hook fastening.

Finger puppets can be stored in clear, labelled video cassette holders. The children will learn to recognize the labels and find their favourite story characters.

Story retelling
Create a set of finger puppets to use with stories during the year. Place the puppets in the story corner so the children can retell their favourite story or make one up.

Storytelling with Puppets, Props and Playful Tales
Written by Mary Jo Huff

Finger puppet playhouse

This playhouse will accommodate many finger puppets – an entire family could live here.

Materials
Large cereal box; spray paint; craft knife; permanent markers.

Directions
Spray paint a wide, tall cereal box. Cut out windows and a door for the puppets to use. Cut a large hole in the back of the box for the children to put their hands through. Use permanent markers to outline where the windows and door are on the back of the box so the storyteller can tell the story and move the puppets more easily. The finger puppets can be stored in the bottom of the box. A town can be created with several boxes and puppets for the houses.

Story retelling
The children can use the playhouse and finger puppets for neighbourhood conversations and storytelling from one house to another. Provide several houses in the story corner and rotate the puppets to develop the children's imaginations.

Finger puppet playhouse

Front

Back

This page may be photocopied by the purchasing institution only.

Brilliant Publications
www.brilliantpublications.co.uk

Storytelling with Puppets, Props and Playful Tales
Written by Mary Jo Huff

Folded paper puppet

Materials

Heavy sugar paper or card in several colours, (23 cm x 30 cm will make a child-size puppet; 30 cm x 46 cm is better for an adult-sized puppet)
Markers
Glue
Scissors
Decorative materials (feathers, buttons, plastic eyes)

Use folded sugar paper to create a fierce 'talking' alligator.

Directions

1. Fold the sugar paper lengthways into three equal parts.

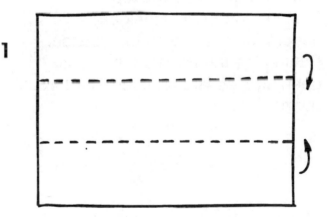

2. With the open side down on the table, fold in half.

3. Fold the top and bottom back to meet in the middle. The open flap is on the inside.

4. Add eyes to distinguish the top of the puppet. In the illustration, white circles and black circles are glued on to create large alligator eyes. White paper zigzag teeth are glued to the open area to create a fierce alligator mouth.

To use the puppet, insert the two middle fingers into the top opening. Keep the index and little fingers for balance on the outside. Putting the thumb into the bottom opening gets you ready to make your puppet talk.

Story retelling

The puppet shown here can be used to retell the story **Mr Alligator and the monkeys** (see page 19). Children can also construct their own story characters to use with other tales or with one they create. After a story has been chosen and a puppet has been made, send home a note to the parents announcing that their child has a special story to tell or retell. This kind of activity will let parents share part of their child's day.

Mr Alligator and the monkeys

Five little monkeys swinging in a tree,
Teasing Mr Alligator – 'You can't catch me!' (high-pitched voice)
Along came Mr Alligator –
Sluuuuuuurrrrrrpppppppppp!

Four little monkeys swinging in a tree,
Teasing Mr Alligator – 'You can't catch me!'
Along came Mr Alligator –
Sluuuuuuurrrrrrpppppppppp!

Three little monkeys swinging in a tree,
Teasing Mr Alligator – 'You can't catch me!'
Along came Mr Alligator –
Sluuuuuuurrrrrrpppppppppp!

Two little monkeys swinging in a tree,
Teasing Mr Alligator – 'You can't catch me!'
Along came Mr Alligator –
Sluuuuuuurrrrrrpppppppppp!

One little monkey swinging in a tree,
Teasing Mr Alligator – 'You can't catch me!'
Along came Mr Alligator –
Sluuuuuuurrrrrrpppppppppp!

That one little monkey swung out of the tree,
And yelled, 'Ha! Ha! Ha! You can't catch me!'

Mr Alligator and the monkeys props

These puppets and props, along with the folded paper alligator, can be used with a story board or story apron for the telling of **Mr Alligator and the monkeys**.

Materials
Art foam (brown and green); hook fastening; scissors; glue.

Directions
Tree – Cut out a tree trunk shape from brown art foam and a rounded top from green art foam. Attach the top and bottom with glue. Cut out holes as indicated. Attach hook fastening. Place on the storytelling apron (page 104) or on the story board (page 110).

Monkeys – Cut out five monkeys from brown art foam using the patterns as a guide. Attach a small piece of hook fastening to each raised paw. Attach the monkeys to the tree where the holes are cut out.

Story retelling
Provide the children with a set of monkeys, a tree, and their own folded paper Mr Alligator puppet. Have them retell the tale of Mr Alligator and the five monkeys or make up their own version.

Brilliant Publications
www.brilliantpublications.co.uk

Storytelling with Puppets, Props and Playful Tales
Written by Mary Jo Huff

Tree pattern

This page may be photocopied by the purchasing institution only.

Glove puppet

Old gloves find new life as chicken, cockerel, and turkey puppets.

Materials
Adult- or child-sized glove; quilt stuffing/padding; dowel; string; glue; decorative materials (wool, feathers, felt, plastic eyes, etc).

Directions
Stuff the glove with quilt padding. Coat one end of the dowel with a generous amount of glue and insert it into the glove. Tie a string tightly around the open end of the glove to enclose the dowel. Leaving only a short length of the dowel extending from the glove will give the puppet a neater appearance. Decorate the puppet to suit the story. This type of puppet works well as a duck, chicken, turkey, cockerel, or any kind of bird.

Story retelling
With a variety of glove puppets in the story corner, children can retell many different stories as well as create their own.

Brilliant Publications
www.brilliantpublications.co.uk

Storytelling with Puppets, Props and Playful Tales
Written by Mary Jo Huff

Hey, Mr Turkey – an interactive chant

Hey, Mr Turkey! (leader)
Hey, Mr Turkey! (child)
Hey, Mr Turkey! (leader)
Hey, Mr Turkey! (child)
Yoo-hoo! yoo-hoo! (leader)

Hey, Mr Turkey! (leader)
Hey, Mr Turkey! (child)
Hey, Mr Turkey! (leader)
Hey, Mr Turkey! (child)
I'm going to catch you! (leader)

Hey, Mr Turkey! (leader)
Hey, Mr Turkey! (child)
Hey, Mr Turkey! (leader)
Hey, Mr Turkey! (child)
Way up in that tree! (leader)

Hey, Mr Turkey! (leader)
Hey, Mr Turkey! (child)
Hey, Mr Turkey! (leader)
Hey, Mr Turkey! (child)
Fly away free! (leader)

Hand puppet

Hand puppets can be an essential part of your curriculum and are fun for children to use. Hand puppets can be made with or without mouths, but puppets with mouths are usually preferable. The following pattern can be adapted to make people or animal-shaped puppets. Encourage the children to use their imaginations to add faces, ears, hair, and clothes.

Materials
Felt; upholstery fabric; loop nylon fabric and hook fastening
Art foam
Laminated card
Glue
Needle and thread
Scissors
Other decorative materials (wool, feathers, and plastic eyes)

Directions
Cut out two pattern shapes using the fabric you choose. Sew or glue them together leaving the bottom open. If you use loop nylon fabric, glue or sew the wrong sides together. This fabric will not fray. Hook fastening can be attached to decorative items to create or change a puppet's personality.

Story retelling
This type of puppet is fun and easy for children to use. Show them how to insert their hand the first time they use one. Keep the puppets in a puppet house in the story corner for the children to use.

Hand puppet patterns

Child size

Shorten or lengthen here

This page may be photocopied by the purchasing institution only.

Brilliant Publications
www.brilliantpublications.co.uk

Storytelling with Puppets, Props and Playful Tales
Written by Mary Jo Huff

Open-mouth talking puppet

A puppet that can open its mouth, talk, and even eat will be an exciting storytelling motivator. Children can turn this pattern into any number of characters.

Materials
Upholstery fabric; fake fur; variety of fabrics (heavy felt or cotton, denim); loop nylon fabric and hook fastening; scissors; pins; sewing machine and thread or fabric glue; decorative materials (wool, plastic eyes, etc).

Directions
Cut out two of body pattern **A** from loop nylon fabric. This fabric will let the puppet be transformed into different characters by simply attaching different heads and tails with hook fastening.

Place the right sides of material together and sew between points 1 – 2. Leave both ends open. The pattern can be extended to make a caterpillar, snake, etc.

Place the mouth pattern **B** on the fold of the material and cut out. Pin pattern **B** inside the mouth pattern **A** and stitch tops together and bottoms together between the point 2's – see diagrams on page 29. Backstitch over the corners or use fabric glue to reinforce them.

Story retelling
Because a talking puppet can talk and eat, it should have a house and some things to munch on. Children can create these different items as well as a variety of headsand tails to use with their puppets. They will be able to use the talking puppets to tell a number of tales as well as create their own characters and stories.

The lion and the mouse

One day, a lion lay fast asleep in a clearing at the edge of the forest. His great mane covered his head and his head rested on his giant paws.

A timid little mouse, on his way home, came scurrying by and bumped into the great animal. Hastily he tried to run away but the lion awakened as the mouse hurried across his mane. With a loud roar the lion grabbed the little mouse in his paw and was ready to eat him.

'Please let me go, spare me!' exclaimed the mouse. 'Some day I will repay you!'

With a laughing roar, the lion let the little mouse go because he had been brave enough to ask for mercy. 'A brave little fellow,' thought the generous lion.

Some days later, the lion was stalking his prey in the deep forest when he was caught in a hunter's net. Unable to get out, the lion roared an angry, loud roar. The little mouse heard the roar and knew it belonged to the lion. He followed the sound of more roars and found the lion tightly trapped in the hunter's net.

'I will help you,' said the little mouse.

'How can you help me?' asked the lion. 'If I cannot tear the ropes loose, no-one can.'

'I told you I would help you some day,' said the mouse. He began to gnaw on the net. He gnawed on the net until the lion was freed.

'Now aren't you sorry you laughed at me when I said I would repay you some day?' asked the mouse. 'Even a tiny little mouse like me can help a great king like you.'

Brilliant Publications
www.brilliantpublications.co.uk

Storytelling with Puppets, Props and Playful Tales
Written by Mary Jo Huff

Body pattern

Child size

Body pattern

A

2   1

2   1

Inside mouth piece

B

Fold

2

2

Place on fold of material

B ⇒ A

This page may be photocopied by the purchasing institution only.

Lion pattern

Use the body pattern with the lion and the mouse puppets.

Lion

Cut out the lion's head and add curly wool to make the mane. Add eyes and a felt nose. Use wool to create a tail. Attach the head and tail to the body with small pieces of hook fastening; this will let you interchange the lion's head and tail with the mouse's.

 Brilliant Publications
www.brilliantpublications.co.uk **Storytelling with Puppets, Props and Playful Tales**
Written by Mary Jo Huff

Mouse pattern

Mouse

Cut out the mouse's head and add a felt nose and whiskers. Twist a pipe cleaner around a pencil to make a curly tail. Attach small pieces of hook fastening to the head and tail to interchange with the lion's head and tail.

Pop-up puppet

A puppet on a dowel stick can sing and dance to music, jump up and down, and even pop out and surprise you.

Materials
Plastic or cardboard sewing cone (the type used on knitting machines) or large funnel; dowel (a size that suits your needs); spray paint or acrylic paint and brush; cotton print fabric; fabric glue; needle and thread; large pompom or Styrofoam ball; glue; scissors; trim or braiding; decorative materials (felt, plastic eyes, etc).

Directions
Spray-paint the cone or brush on acrylic paint. place the cone pattern on the fold of the material and cut out. Glue or sew together the sides with the wrong sides facing out. Leave the bottom open. Glue or sew on the paws, hands, etc.

When the glue has dried, turn the puppet body right-side out. Now dab glue on the end of the dowel and push the dowel into the puppet body. Squeeze the material around the end of the dowel. Dab glue on the bottom of the pompom or Styrofoam ball and press it over the end of the fabric-covered dowel.

Let the glue dry for several hours. When dry, add eyes, ears, mouth, etc, to the pompom to suit the character. Place the dowel through the large end of the painted cone and glue the bottom of the fabric to the cone. Cover the edge where the fabric meets the cone by gluing on trim or braiding. Decorate as desired.

Story retelling
Put various pop-up puppets in the story corner and let the children tell their own stories. Their imaginations will soar as different pop-up characters are discovered in the centre.

Storytelling with Puppets, Props and Playful Tales
Written by Mary Jo Huff

Pop-up patterns

Place on fold of
material

Cone cover

This page may be photocopied by the purchasing institution only.

This page may be photocopied by the purchasing institution only.

Brilliant Publications
www.brilliantpublications.co.uk

Storytelling with Puppets, Props and Playful Tales
Written by Mary Jo Huff

Sock puppet

Sock puppets are expressive and easy to make. They can also live in a variety of houses, such as large tin cans, boxes, and tubes.

Materials
Old socks (tube socks works very well); glue; marker; decorative materials (plastic eyes, pieces of felt, etc).

Directions
Try to make this puppet out of a sock that fits your hand. Place your hand inside the sock, open your hand, and push the sock between your thumb and fingers. This space is the mouth. Mark spots to add eyes, hair, tongue, etc, to create the particular story character.

For two puppets in one – good to use with two characters who talk back and forth or for a character that metamorphoses – place one sock inside another and stitch or glue the cuffs together. Decorate as desired.

Story retelling
The sock puppet can live in a playhouse made from a large tin can, a box, or a tube. Sock puppets are also particularly good for retelling stories about worms, snakes, or caterpillars, like the story **The Very Hungry Caterpillar by Eric Carle**. Place a sock puppet and its house in the story corner and listen to the children retell stories and create their own.

Sock puppet in a tin

Permanently attaching a sock puppet into a tin can home makes it durable as well as eye-catching. Just be sure metal edges are smooth to the touch.

Materials

A large, empty tin can (eg for formula milk) with both ends removed; heavy tape or duct tape; two plastic lids that fit the tin can; spray paint or acrylic paint and brush; glue; sock puppet; vinyl letters.

Directions

Clean the tin inside and out. Be sure the edges are smooth to the touch. If not, cover with heavy tape or duct tape. Be sure the plastic lids fit tight so you can store the puppet once the puppet has been put inside. Paint the tin. When dry, glue your favourite sock puppet inside. Let the glue dry completely. Then glue on vinyl letters to give the puppet a name.

When the puppet is used for play, the tin can lids should be removed so the child can get a hand inside the sock. To store, press the puppet down inside the tin and cover with the plastic lids.

Story retelling

Let the children manipulate the puppet in its house. If the puppet is placed in the story centre, the children will use it to help retell their favourite stories.

Stick puppet

Stick puppets are versatile – they can be short or tall, large or little, and pop out of houses or live on their own.

Materials

Heavy paper or art foam
Glue
Laminator
Markers or paint
Scissors
Ice lolly stick, tongue depressor or paint stirrer
Tape
Self-adhesive hook fastening or magnet

Directions

Draw and colour a puppet shape on heavy paper and laminate. Or colour a puppet pattern, laminate, and glue to a larger piece of art foam. For a small puppet, glue the picture to an ice lolly stick; for a larger puppet, glue it to a tongue depressor or paint stirrer.

If you want to make puppet pictures inter-changeable, tape a heavy piece of paper to the back of the art foam or laminated paper and leave the bottom open. Insert the stick into this tunnel for puppet use, and remove to use with a different puppet.

To use a stick puppet with a story board or magnetic board, remove the stick and add a small piece of hook fastening or a self-adhesive magnet.

Story retelling

Stick puppet characters can be housed in a tin can or a box and lend themselves for use with many stories.

Down by the pond

Down by the pond where the catkins grow,
Back to my boat I dare not go.
For if I do my grandpa will say,
'Did you ever see a fish
Eating from a dish, down by the pond?'

Down by the pond where the catkins grow,
Back to my boat I dare not go.
For if I do my grandpa will say,
'Did you ever see a snake
Licking a cake, down by the pond?'

Down by the pond where the catkins grow,
Back to my boat I dare not go.
For if I do my grandpa will say,
'Did you ever see a raccoon
Smiling at the moon, down by the pond?'

Down by the pond where the catkins grow,
Back to my boat I dare not go.
For if I do my grandpa will say,
'Did you ever see a frog
Kissing a dog, down by the pond?'

Down by the pond where the catkins grow,
Back to my boat I dare not go.
For if I do my grandpa will say,
'Did you ever try to rhyme
In the warm sunshine, down by the pond?'

Storytelling with Puppets, Props and Playful Tales
Written by Mary Jo Huff

Stick puppet patterns

Copy patterns on to heavy paper, colour, cut out, laminate, and glue sticks to the back. Use with the **Down by the pond** tale (see page 38).

Fish

Dish

This page may be photocopied by the purchasing institution only.

Snake

Cake

This page may be photocopied by the purchasing institution only.

Brilliant Publications
www.brilliantpublications.co.uk

Storytelling with Puppets, Props and Playful Tales
Written by Mary Jo Huff

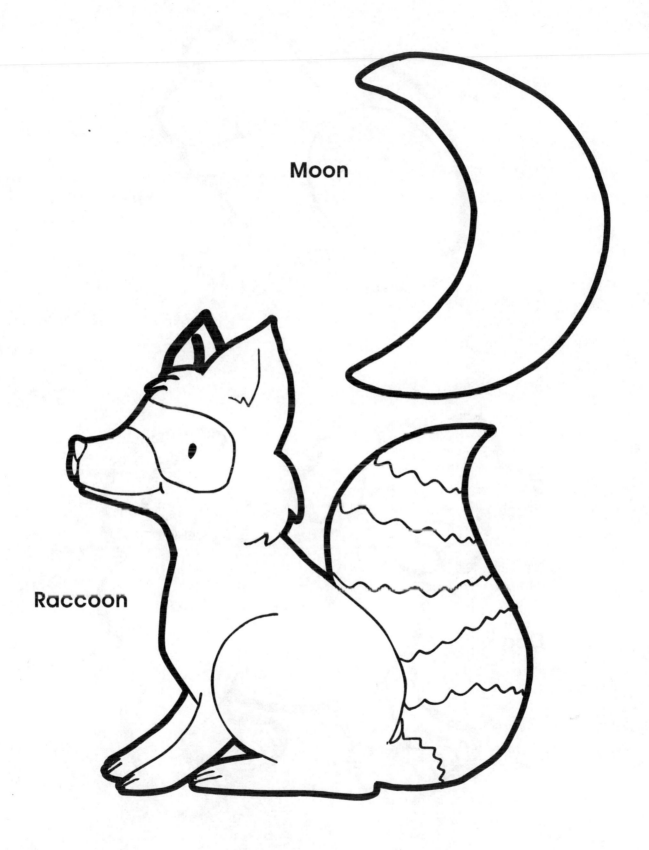

Moon

Raccoon

Storytelling with Puppets, Props and Playful Tales
Written by Mary Jo Huff

Brilliant Publications
www.brilliantpublications.co.uk

Frog

Dog

This page may be photocopied by the purchasing institution only.

Brilliant Publications
www.brilliantpublications.co.uk

Storytelling with Puppets, Props and Playful Tales
Written by Mary Jo Huff

Tube puppet

A variety of tubes and materials can be used to make these story puppets. Kitchen towel tubes, tin foil or cling film tubes are ideal for children to use as bases. When the puppets are ready to go home, you can attach a note that tells the parents about the story the child has chosen and the puppet he or she has made. Encourage family members to ask the child to retell the story using the puppet.

Materials
Cardboard tubes;
Markers
Paint and brushes
Scissors
Glue
Art foam
Wiggly eyes
Felt and pompoms
Paper baking cases
A variety of decorative materials
Coloured sugar paper and tissue paper

Directions
Let the children paint and then glue decorative materials to their cardboard tubes to represent favourite story characters. Tube puppets can represent people, animals, or fantasy figures.

Story retelling
Provide the children with a favourite book and a special tube puppet character to retell the story with. Children may also want to use the puppets they make to put on a puppet show.

Tube puppet ideas

This page may be photocopied by the purchasing institution only.

Brilliant Publications
www.brilliantpublications.co.uk

Storytelling with Puppets, Props and Playful Tales
Written by Mary Jo Huff

Commercial puppets

Commercial puppets are available through many educational shops, toy shops and catalogues. Purchasing a special puppet can enhance your story corner elsewhere. Child-size puppets are available and can enrich a child's story appreciation. But don't purchase a puppet just because it's sweet and appealing. Only buy one if it will support your storytelling curriculum.

Commercial puppets range in size from tiny finger puppets to very large puppets. When you buy a puppet, always be sure that it fits your hand and is easy to manipulate. Work the puppet's mouth, check that the head turns and see if it fits both your hand and arm comfortably.

The following are a few of the types of commercial puppets available.

People puppets

Interchangeable people puppets are favourites because they are so easy to manipulate. One puppet can double as many others with just a change of outfit. People puppets come in different skin tones and with many changes of clothes.

Animal puppets

There are many appealing life-like wild animals available. These include foxes, rabbits, raccoons, even ring-tailed lemurs.

Television characters

The most easily available puppets in toy shops are characters from children's television shows. Apart from **Sooty and Co**, these are from the popular programmes **Sesame Street**, **Winnie the Pooh**, **Barney** and even the **Rugrats**.

Props and playful tales

Storytelling with props

Props are an enhancement to any story corner and invite the children to get ready to hear and tell a good story. Props give children clues to what the forthcoming story will focus on and can also be used to start a conversation about a story, for example, 'Looking at this honey jar, what do you think the story is about?' Props also help to develop language, listening and speaking skills. Props will also help explain images and words contained in stories.

Props also encourage children to participate in a story, both as listeners and as speakers in retelling. As you choose stories to tell, look for those that encourage participation. Workable props can be found at almost any type of shop: supermarkets, hardware, craft, school-supply and specialist shops, as well as hotel and museum gift shops. Many of the small items we use on a daily basis can also be recycled as props or used in prop creations children make for favourite stories. The props detailed in this section may motivate you to come up with additional ideas of your own.

If you and the children enjoy telling stories with a story board, prop cutouts can be made from felt, art foam, paper, magazine pictures, or hand-drawn images with a piece of hook fastening attached to the back. Keeping a story board in the story corner will encourage children to manipulate the figures and think about stories in different ways.

  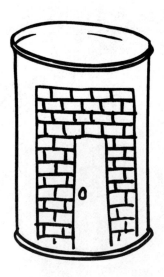

Story-starters

Story-starters are special tools for signalling the beginning of storytelling time. A story-starter, such as a song or chant, a special prop, or a class mascot will invite the children to gather together.

One good story-starter to try is this simple chant:

Story-time chant
Hey, hey, what do you say?
Hey, hey, what do you say?
Hey, hey, what do you say?
I have a story for you today!

Hey, hey, what do you say?
Hey, hey, what do you say?
Hey, hey, what do you say?
Now it's time for story play.

Story-starter puppets
Below and on the following pages are some examples of character story-starters that can be made from inexpensive and easily purchased materials. Use these examples as a springboard for your own creativity.

Larry Lion
Mop-head replacements can be purchased at supermarkets and hardware stores. They have two holes in the back where your fingers can be inserted for easy manipulation. The eyes are made with large pompoms, the nose from a medium-sized pompom and the mouth from a piece of art foam.

Story-starter puppets

Madame Belinda and Madame Melinda
These items (a plastic bottle and window wiper) can be purchased at supermarkets and hardware shops. Add two eyes, a nose, and a mouth cut from art foam, some curly wool hair, and a small hat purchased at a craft shop. Using a high-pitched voice with these story-starters is very effective.

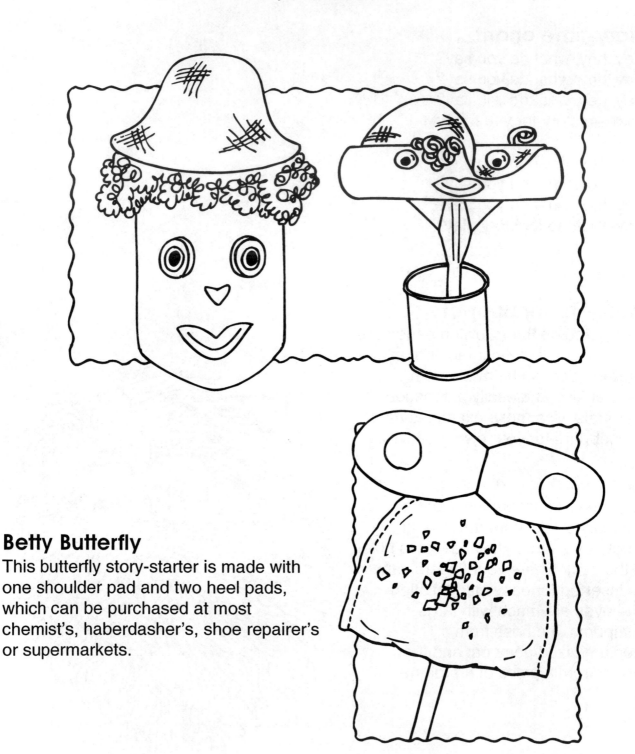

Betty Butterfly
This butterfly story-starter is made with one shoulder pad and two heel pads, which can be purchased at most chemist's, haberdasher's, shoe repairer's or supermarkets.

Brilliant Publications
www.brilliantpublications.co.uk

Storytelling with Puppets, Props and Playful Tales
Written by Mary Jo Huff

Mop people

Mop people are excellent motivators for storytelling participation. The mop person on the left is Peter Pirate; the one on the right is Ms Mary Mop. Small mops can be found at supermarkets and hardware shops.

Fancy Nancy

This cute story-starter is made from a dowel, a Styrofoam ball, a small mop-head replacement, a straw hat, and earrings, all of which can be purchased at a craft shop or hardware shop. The face is drawn on with a permanent marker.

Dishpan Dan

Dishpan Dan is made out of a small
kitchen mop for washing dishes.
Wiggly eyes and some curly wool hair
have been glued on, and a nose and
mouth added with paint.

Molly Mop

Molly is a mop-head replacement with pompom eyes and nose and a mouth made
from a piece of red, glued-on art foam. Beads have been strung throughout Molly's
hair, a project the children can undertake. Children may wish to continue to
experiment with this story-starter's hair decorations.

Dandy Dusters

The characters shown here are just a few of the low-cost feather duster story-starters you can create. Use your imagination to add eyes, nose, mouth, hair, hat, and clothes.

Coach Butch

This story-starter is a good one for introducing the children to stories about competition. The coach's hair is part of the mop head, and his face is drawn on with a permanent marker. A piece of foam board cut into an oval can be glued to the mop handle.

Fluff and Puff

Fluff and Puff are made from kitchen mops. Puff has two ping-pong balls for eyes on which black centres have been drawn with a permanent marker. Fluff's eyes are made from two medium-sized pompoms and the nose and mouth are drawn on a plastic bottle top. A soft, slow voice is effective for use with Puff and a high-pitched, whiny voice with Fluff.

Redhead Man

This story-starter is made from a red, two-sided lint brush. Both sides look alike except on one there is a smile and on the other a frown. The hair is made from three large multi-coloured pompoms, the eyes from wiggly eyes, and the other features from art foam. Redhead Man's tie and decorations are also cut from art foam.

Caterpillar-to-butterfly props

When metamorphosis is part of the story, these props help in the telling and retelling.

Materials

1 green paint roller; 3 green pipe cleaners; 1 black pipe cleaner; 2 white table tennis balls; 2 wiggly eyes; glue; scissors; paper towel roll; green sugar paper; several shades of green tissue paper; green tape; black felt; white paper coffee filter; non-pinch-style clothes pegs; markers; squirt bottle; water.

Directions

Caterpillar

Space out the three green pipe cleaners and glue them around the paint roller to make the roller look as if it's segmented. Glue the two ping-pong balls and the wiggly eyes to the front of the body. Bend the black pipe cleaner in half and add for antennae. The version 2 butterfly can be rolled up and stored inside the caterpillar.

Butterfly 1

Cover the paper towel roll with green sugar paper. Cut out and glue on black felt eyes and glue on layers of green tissue paper for wings.

Butterfly 2

Use markers to add colours or designs to the coffee filter. Squirt with water and let dry. Crumple the filter slightly and insert into the clothes peg. Fluff out the tissue paper wings. Add colour or drawings to the clothes peg body if desired. The completed butterfly can be stored inside the paint roller caterpillar to emerge at the appropriate time.

Story retelling

Children can create individual caterpillar and butterfly props to take home to share with their families. Attach a note to the props encouraging parents to listen to their child's story and to read a suggested story together. In the story corner, provide caterpillar and butterfly props and a copy of **The Very Hungry Caterpillar by Eric Carle**.

Patterns

Caterpillar

Butterfly 2

This page may be photocopied by the pzurchasing institution only.

Brilliant Publications
www.brilliantpublications.co.uk

Storytelling with Puppets, Props and Playful Tales
Written by Mary Jo Huff

Large tin can houses

Basic construction
A large tin can makes a durable puppet house. Use these tins to store puppets and props in the story corner.

Materials
A large empty tin can with a plastic lid (eg for formula milk)
Heavy tape or duct tape
Paint primer
Spray paint
Permanent markers or acrylic paint and brushes
Clear sealer

Directions
Clean the tin can. Cover rough edges with heavy tape or duct tape. Paint the can with primer and let dry. Then paint the tin the desired colour.

If you're making a house for a particular puppet or story, add art work to fit the story. When dry, label the tin, spray it with a clear sealer, and fill with puppets or props. Cover with the plastic lid.

Story retelling
Place the tin can houses in the story corner and rotate them.

The three little pigs' houses

  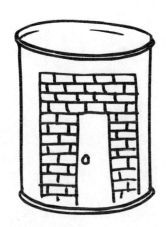

Nursery rhyme prop cans

This page may be photocopied by the purchasing institiution only.

Brilliant Publications
www.brilliantpublications.co.uk

Storytelling with Puppets, Props and Playful Tales
Written by Mary Jo Huff

Festival prop cans

This page may be photocopied by the purchasing institiution only.

Theme prop cans

Outer
space

Sea life

Honey jar

Log

This page may be photocopied by the purchasing institution only.

Brilliant Publications
www.brilliantpublications.co.uk

Storytelling with Puppets, Props and Playful Tales
Written by Mary Jo Huff

Who stole the honey?

Let the children make art foam puppets from the patterns on the following pages. Puppets with magnets can be manipulated on the Honey jar tin can (see page 60).

Who stole the honey from the honey jar?

'Who stole the honey from the honey jar?'

'**FOX** stole the honey from the honey jar.'
'Who me?'
'Yeah, you!'
'Not me!'
'Then who?'

'**BADGER** stole the honey from the honey jar.'
'Who me?'
'Yeah, you!'
'Not me!'
'Then who?'

'**RABBIT** stole the honey from the honey jar.'
'Who me?'
'Yeah, you!'
'Not me!'
'Then who?'

'**SQUIRREL** stole the honey from the honey jar.'
'Who me?'
'Yeah, you!'
'Not me!'
Then who?'

'**BEAR** stole the honey from the honey jar.'
'Who me?'
'Yeah, you!'
'Yeah, me!
I took the honey from the honey jar.
Yum! Yum! Yum!'

Patterns

Fox

Badger

This page may be photocopied by the purchasing institution only.

Brilliant Publications
www.brilliantpublications.co.uk

Storytelling with Puppets, Props and Playful Tales
Written by Mary Jo Huff

Squirrel

Rabbit

This page may be photocopied by the purchasing institution only.

Bear

This page may be photocopied by the purchasing institution only.

Brilliant Publications
www.brilliantpublications.co.uk

Storytelling with Puppets, Props and Playful Tales
Written by Mary Jo Huff

Small tin can houses and puppets

Children can create their own storytelling houses and characters using a variety of small tin cans. An adult may be required to paint on the base coat before the children begin.

Materials
Assorted small tin cans with plastic lids
Heavy tape or duct tape
Paint primer
Spray paint or acrylic paint and brushes
Clear sealer
Art items (art foam, wiggly eyes, wool, felt, buttons, feathers)

Directions
Clean the tin inside and out and remove the label. Brush on primer. Then paint the tin the desired colour. If the tin will be used as a puppet, add features like those of a favourite story character. If acrylic paint is used, coat when dry with a clear sealer. Use art foam for adding arms and legs.

Story retelling
Mix these small tin can houses and puppets with the large tin can houses in the story corner to create interest. The props and puppets will aid in a wide variety of story retelling.

Small tin can house ideas

Soup tin bunny

Small tin frog

Crisps tube king

This page may be photocopied by the purchasing institution only.

Brilliant Publications
www.brilliantpublications.co.uk

Storytelling with Puppets, Props and Playful Tales
Written by Mary Jo Huff

Circle time props

When it's circle time, these props can help children take it in turns creating a story.

Materials

An empty small tin can
Spray paint
Wooden spoons (one for each child)
Non-toxic clear spray sealer
Permanent markers

Directions

Spray paint the tin. Spray the spoons with clear sealer. Then let the children draw a picture of their face on the back of a spoon and print their name on the inside bowl. Place all the spoons in the tin and keep in the story corner.

Storytelling

Encourage the children to find their spoons and gather for circle time. Remind the children to keep their spoons in their laps while others are speaking. Begin the story by saying, 'Once upon a time…'

Pass the story from one spoon storyteller to another. Children can hold up their spoons when they are telling the story. Be sure that each child gets a chance to add to the story.

Collect the spoons and return them to the tin.

Story retelling

The children can take their spoons home over a holiday break. When they return to school, let each child take a turn telling about his or her holiday adventures. The spoons can also be used at home for child/parent storytelling. Send a note home with each spoon to encourage the sharing of a special story.

Copier paper box house

Copier paper boxes make excellent puppet houses. They're roomy and sturdy and their lids can become roofs.

Materials
Empty copier paper box
Spray paint or acrylic paint and brushes
Permanent markers

Directions
Paint the box a suitable colour for a house in a favourite story. The lid can be painted a contrasting colour. Use permanent markers to add features such as windows, doors, window boxes, front door lights, and roof tiles.

Story retelling
When kept in the story corner, copier paper box houses can be used for story retelling. Houses can also store a variety of small puppets and props.

Pillowcase house

For a puppet house that's soft to the touch as well as easy to move around, a pillowcase does the trick.

Materials
Pillowcase; sponges; paint.

Directions
Let the children take turns sponge-painting the pillowcase to resemble a house from a favourite story. Let it dry thoroughly before putting it to use.

Story retelling
This soft, flexible house can be moved to different locations as the children retell a story. Puppets and story props can be stored inside.

Pillowcase ideas

Sun

Farm

Ocean

Space

Dinosaurs

Brilliant Publications
www.brilliantpublications.co.uk

Storytelling with Puppets, Props and Playful Tales
Written by Mary Jo Huff

Shoe box house

A shoe box can be transformed into a puppet house that's just the right size for small hands to put figures into. Shoe boxes can also be turned into puppets or story props.

Materials
Large shoe box; sponges and paint or acrylic paint and brushes; permanent markers; glue; scissors; art items (wool, art foam, felt, wiggly eyes, and cotton wool balls)

Directions
Paint the box an appropriate colour for the story; sponge-painting works very well on this surface. If the box will be used as a house, add features with markers or pens. Windows and doors can be cut out or partially cut to open. If the box will be used as a puppet or prop, glue on any necessary materials.

Story retelling
Set the box and its storybook in the story corner. Encourage the children to use it as they retell the story. Puppets and props can be stored inside.

Aesop's fable box

The playful frog props

Materials
Large tin can (eg for formula milk)
Spray paint
Acrylic paint and brushes
Permanent markers

Directions
Paint the tin to look like a pond scene, with a frog sitting on a log. Label the tin with the title of its tale. The story props can be housed in the tin.

Story retelling
Encourage the children to use the puppets and props with the pond scene to retell the story. The story can also be retold using commercially made props. Plastic or rubber caterpillars, fish, and frogs can be purchased at most school-supply or toy shops.
If the mosquitoes make a loud buzzing sound when the story is originally told, the children will want to retell it many times. Once you have taught the children the repeated verse, they will want to come up with their own versions.

Brilliant Publications
www.brilliantpublications.co.uk

Storytelling with Puppets, Props and Playful Tales
Written by Mary Jo Huff

The playful frog
by Mary Jo Huff

Once upon a time, a little frog was sitting quietly on a big old log. It was time for lunch and the frog was really hungry. He noticed a small lizard sunning himself on the end of the log. He hopped over to the lizard and said:

> I'm a hungry little frog.
> And you're bothering my log.
> I don't want to fight,
> But if you don't watch out,
> I'll just take a bite.

The hungry frog flicked out his quick tongue and gobbled up that little lizard.

But the frog was STILL hungry. He looked around and saw a fuzzy caterpillar crawling up the side of the log. He hopped over to the caterpillar and said:

> I'm a hungry little frog.
> And you're bothering my log.
> I don't want to fight,
> But if you don't watch out,
> I'll just take a bite.

With a quick flick of his tongue, the hungry frog gobbled up that fuzzy caterpillar.

But the frog was STILL hungry. He spotted a dragonfly resting on the end of the log. He hopped over to the dragonfly and said:

> I'm a hungry little frog.
> And you're bothering my log.
> I don't want to fight,
> But if you don't watch out,
> I'll just take a bite.

The frog's tongue was quicker than the wings of the dragonfly, and the frog gobbled the dragonfly up.

But the little frog was STILL hungry. He heard a swarm of mosquitoes hovering close to the top of the log. He quietly hopped near the swarm and said:

> I'm a hungry little frog.
> And you're bothering my log.
> I don't want to fight,
> But if you don't watch out,
> I'll just take a bite.

Before the swarm could move, the frog swallowed every one of the mosquitoes with one quick flick of his tongue.

But the little frog was STILL hungry. A small fish swam close to the log. The little frog hopped up to the fish and said:

> I'm a hungry little frog.
> And you're bothering my log.
> I don't want to fight,
> But if you don't watch out,
> I'll just take a bite.

That little fish laughed and dared the frog to take a bite. The frog leaped towards the little fish but the fish swam away and hid behind some rocks. The little frog swam after the fish but could not find him. As the frog searched for the little fish, along came a **big fish**, who looked at the little frog and said:

> I'm a **big old fish**
> With a hungry wish.
> I don't want to fight,
> But if you don't watch out,
> I'll just take a bite.

The frightened little frog swam to the top of the water and leaped upon his log. He was grateful to be a quiet little frog, just sitting on his log.

Brilliant Publications
www.brilliantpublications.co.uk

Storytelling with Puppets, Props and Playful Tales
Written by Mary Jo Huff

Patterns

The following patterns can be used to create puppets and props out of art foam. Adding hook fastening to each completed pattern will make it suitable for use with a loop nylon story board or storytelling apron. Adding a magnet to each piece will enable it to be used on the tin can house or on a magnetic board.

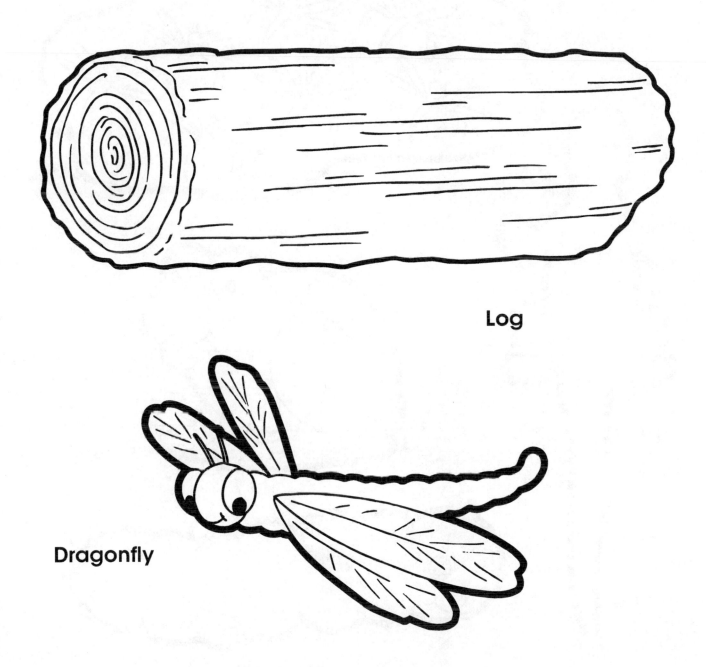

Log

Dragonfly

This page may be photocopied by the purchasing institution only.

Mosquito swarm

Frog

Lizard

Caterpillar

This page may be photocopied by the purchasing institution only.

Brilliant Publications
www.brilliantpublications.co.uk

Storytelling with Puppets, Props and Playful Tales
Written by Mary Jo Huff

Little fish

Big fish

This page may be photocopied by the purchasing institution only.

Gingerbread Man props

This imaginative story will be hard for children to resist.

Materials

2 sturdy white paper plates
6 metal spatulas
Art foam
Stapler
Scissors
Self-adhesive magnets
Brown paint (watercolour, tempera, or acrylic)
Brush
Markers

Directions

Cut characters from art foam and outline features with permanent marker. Add a magnetic square to the back of each character. Paint the paper plates brown. When dry, cut one in half. Staple one half to the full plate to form a pocket for storing the characters. Glue the Gingerbread Man pattern to the front of the paper plate.

Story retelling

Store the Gingerbread Man, puppets and spatulas in the story corner. As the children retell this tale, have them place each character on a spatula as it enters the story. The magnets will keep the puppets on the spatulas. As the children participate in the story retelling, record their versions on cassettes.

Brilliant Publications
www.brilliantpublications.co.uk

Storytelling with Puppets, Props and Playful Tales
Written by Mary Jo Huff

Gingerbread Man
adapted by Mary Jo Huff

There once was an old woman, an old man and their daughter. They all lived on a farm near a big river. One morning, the old woman decided to make a Gingerbread Man for the family. She wanted to teach her daughter the recipe.

'Oh, goody!' exclaimed the little girl. 'This Gingerbread Man will taste delicious!'

The young girl and the old woman rolled the dough out thinly, cut out a Gingerbread Man and put it in the oven to bake. The old woman warned her daughter not to open the oven door until the Gingerbread Man was properly baked.

The old woman went outside to help the old man feed the animals. The little girl smelled the Gingerbread Man and decided to take just a little peek. She opened the oven door just a tiny bit, and the Gingerbread Man rolled out. 'Stop! Stop! Come back!' yelled the little girl.

The Gingerbread Man rolled out the door, across the porch, and down the barnyard path. The old woman, the old man, and their daughter ran after the Gingerbread Man as fast as they could run.

'Run, run, as fast as you can, you can't catch me, I'm the Gingerbread Man.'

Soon the Gingerbread Man came upon a PIG. 'Why are you running away?' asked the pig.

'I've run away from the old woman,
the old man, and their daughter,
and I can run away from you,'
said the Gingerbread Man.

'You think so?' said the pig. And the pig began to chase the Gingerbread Man.

'Run, run, as fast as you can, you can't catch me, I'm the Gingerbread Man.'

The old woman, the old man, the young daughter and the pig all ran fast, but they could not catch him. Soon the Gingerbread Man came upon a Cow in the field. 'Why are you running away?' asked the cow.

'I've run away from the old woman, the old man, the daughter and the pig and I can run away from you too,' said the Gingerbread Man.

'Oh, you think so!' said the cow, and the cow ran fast, but she could not catch the Gingerbread Man .

'Run, run, as fast as you can, you can't catch me, I'm the Gingerbread Man.'

The Gingerbread Man ran past a HORSE galloping in the field. 'Why are you running away?' asked the horse.

'I've run away from the old woman, the old man, the daughter, the pig and the cow, and now I am going to run away from you,' said the Gingerbread Man.

'Oh, you think so!' said the horse, and he began to chase the Gingerbread Man.

'Run, run, as fast as you can, you can't catch me, I'm the Gingerbread Man.'

Brilliant Publications
www.brilliantpublications.co.uk

Storytelling with Puppets, Props and Playful Tales
Written by Mary Jo Huff

The horse ran fast, but he could not catch the Gingerbread Man. Soon the Gingerbread Man met a FOX getting a drink at the river.

'Why are you running away?' asked the fox.

'I've run away from the old woman, the old man, the daughter, the pig, the cow, and the horse, and now I will run away from you,' said the Gingerbread Man.

'How will you cross the river?' asked the sly fox.

'I don't know,' said the Gingerbread Man.

'Hop on my back and I will take you across the river,' the fox told him.

The Gingerbread Man rolled up onto the fox's back and they began to cross the river. As the river deepened, the Gingerbread Man rolled up the fox's back until he was on top of the fox's head. The sly fox raised his head and the Gingerbread Man rolled down his nose and right into the fox's mouth.

The Gingerbread Man ran away from the old woman, the old man, the daughter, the pig, the cow, and the horse, but he did not run away from the sly old fox.

Since all Gingerbread Men are made to be eaten, the fox had the best snack of all.

Patterns

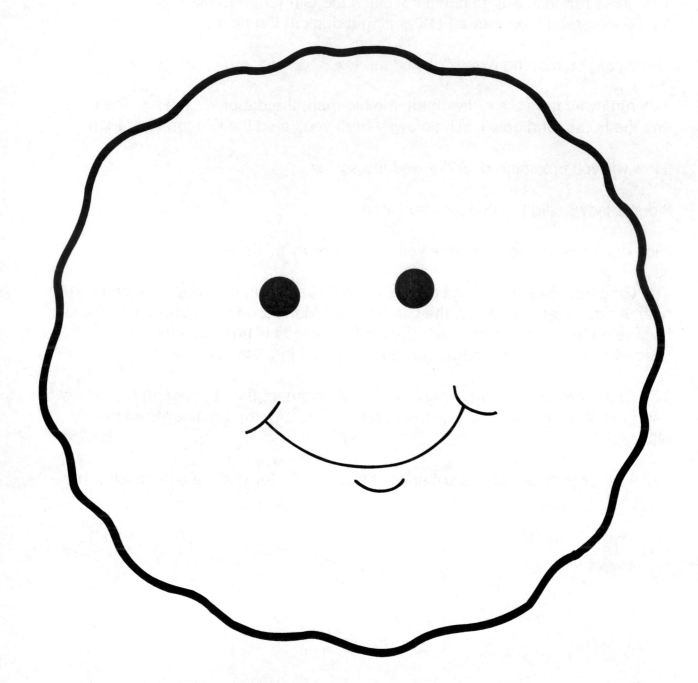

Gingerbread Man

Brilliant Publications
www.brilliantpublications.co.uk

Storytelling with Puppets, Props and Playful Tales
Written by Mary Jo Huff

Old man

Old woman

Girl

Cow

Brilliant Publications
www.brilliantpublications.co.uk

Storytelling with Puppets, Props and Playful Tales
Written by Mary Jo Huff

Fox

Pig

Horse

This page may be photocopied by the purchasing institution only.

The mouse house props

Glove puppets and a small tin can house add to the fun of telling very interactive stories.

Materials
Small tin can; paint; brushes; 1 grey glove and 1 white or black glove; wiggly eyes (tiny and big); wool for tails; fishing line; grey felt; art foam; glue; scissors; heavy cloth or duct tape.

Directions
House – Paint the small can and cut out a mouse hole. Tape over rough edges.

Mice – Use the grey glove for the five mice. Add wiggly eyes and a wool tail to each mouse. Add felt noses and fishing-line whiskers.

Cat – Use a white or black glove that fits your hand. The fingers will point down and be the cat's paws. The thumb will be the tail. On the body of the glove, glue on eyes, an art foam nose and ears, and fishing-line whiskers.

When the cat enters the story, twirl the thumb tail as it approaches the mice. Hold up all five fingers to show how many mice live in the hole. Hold up one finger when the mouse shouts, 'Scat!' Wiggle all five fingers when the mice scurry back to their house.

Story retelling
Keep the mouse house and the glove puppets in the story corner for acting out this cat and mouse story.

Brilliant Publications
www.brilliantpublication.co.uk

Storytelling with Puppets, Props and Playful Tales
Written by Mary Jo Huff

The mouse house

by Mary Jo Huff

Five little mice were hiding in a hole
Waiting to nibble from a dinner bowl.

When it was dark and every light was out
One little mouse could be heard to shout:

'Dinner is served, let's all scurry!'
The cat might come, so the mice had to hurry.

A lookout was chosen to spot the cat.
The others all ate, until they heard, 'SCAT, SCAT!'

The warning was loud, announcing cat trouble,
And five little mice disappeared on the double.

Those furry fat mice gathered back in their hole,
Bellies all full from the dinner bowl.

The farmer's headache props

The children will love to make the animal sounds that bring this farmyard story to life. The story can be told using a pizza box lid as a story board or with a storytelling apron. The pizza box may be used for many other types of stories.

Materials

Medium or large pizza box
Paint (spray paint works best)
Fabric glue
Loop nylon fabric and hook fastening
Markers
Scissors
Art foam

Directions

Spray-paint the pizza box. Cut a square of the loop nylon fabric to fit inside the box lid and glue it on. Let the glue dry completely. Copy the patterns, lay them on top of the art foam, and cut them out. Outline the characters.

Attach a small piece of hook fastening to the back of each character. Store all the characters in the pizza box and use the inside lid for telling the story. Label the box with pictures so the children who cannot read can recognize the story.

Story retelling

Provide the children with the pizza box and the story characters. Two children can retell the story by attaching each character to the box's inside lid as it enters the story.

Brilliant Publications
www.brilliantpublication.co.uk

Storytelling with Puppets, Props and Playful Tales
Written by Mary Jo Huff

The farmer's headache
by Mary Jo Huff

There was a farmer who had a headache because his children were so noisy. He decided to go to his doctor and get a remedy for his throbbing headache.

The doctor told the farmer to get himself a horse and to bring the horse into the house. The farmer went out to the pasture and found a horse and brought the horse back to the house. But the noise from the horse (NEIGHHH!) was too loud.

The farmer returned to the doctor for a new remedy. This time the doctor said to get a cow. The farmer went home and brought a cow into the house. The noise from the cow (MOOOO!) was more than he could bear.

'THE HORSE WENT NEIGHHH!' (children)
'THE COW WENT MOOOOO!' (children)

The farmer returned to the doctor for a new remedy. This time the doctor told the farmer to get a pig. The farmer brought a pig into the house, but the noise the pig made was unbearable. That pig went OINNNNNK! all day long.

'THE HORSE WENT NEIGHHH!' (children)
'THE COW WENT MOOOOO!' (children)
'THE PIG WENT OINNNNNK!' (children)

The farmer went back to the doctor for a better remedy. The doctor said to bring a dog into the house. The farmer followed the doctor's orders and brought the dog into the house. The dog barked all day and evening (WOOFFFFF!).

'THE HORSE WENT NEIGHHH!' (children)
'THE COW WENT MOOOOO!' (children)
'THE PIG WENT OINNNNNK!' (children)
'THE DOG WENT WOOFFFFF!' (children)

This went on all day and all night. The farmer could not get any peace and quiet. He returned to the doctor for a new remedy and the doctor told him to get a cat. So, the farmer brought the cat into the house. That cat screeched MIAOWWW! and the dog chased her around and around the house.

'THE HORSE WENT NEIGHHH!' (children)
'THE COW WENT MOOOOO!' (children)
'THE PIG WENT OINNNNNK!' (children)
'THE DOG WENT WOOFFFFF!' (children)
'THE CAT WENT MIAOWWW!' (children)

The farmer decided to ask the doctor just one more time. The doctor shrugged and suggested the farmer get a quiet mouse. So the farmer brought a tiny little mouse into the house. The cat heard the mouse squeeeeking and said 'MIAOWWW!' (children), the dog heard the cat and began to 'WOOFFFFF' (children), the pig heard the dog and began to 'OINNNNNK!' (children), the cow heard the pig and began to 'MOOOOO!' (children), and the horse heard the commotion and began to 'NEIGHHH!' (children).

All the noise was too much for the farmer, so he put all the animals into the barnyard and enjoyed the quiet of his farmhouse. All he could hear were the sweet voices of his children and wife. The animals stayed in the barnyard and the farmer never had a headache again.

Patterns

Farmer

Horse

Cow

Pig

This page may be photocopied by the purchasing institution only.

Brilliant Publications
www.brilliantpublication.co.uk

Storytelling with Puppets, Props and Playful Tales
Written by Mary Jo Huff

Dog

Cat

Mouse

This page may be photocopied by the purchasing institution only.

Five little speckled frogs props

The story of the little speckled frogs will invite children to jump right in and participate.

Materials
A large empty tin can (eg for formula milk)
Brown spray paint
Black paint and brush
Green art foam
Self-adhesive magnets
Scissors
Marker

Directions
Paint the tin can brown. When dry, spatter it with black paint to resemble a log. Cut out five frogs from the art foam and add a magnet to the back of each. Use a marker to add specks to the frogs. When you tell the story, begin with all five frogs on the log and take one off at a time.

Story retelling
Provide the children with the tin can log with the art foam frogs stored inside. Let them invent their own ways to retell this simple story.

Brilliant Publications
www.brilliantpublication.co.uk

Storytelling with Puppets, Props and Playful Tales
Written by Mary Jo Huff

Five little speckled frogs

Five little speckled frogs,
Sitting on a hollow log,
Eating a most delicious meal.

One jumped into the creek,
The other frogs all said EEEK!
Now there were … (pause)
Just four speckled frogs.

Four little speckled frogs,
Sitting on a hollow log,
Eating a most delicious meal.

One jumped into the creek,
The other frogs all said EEEK!
Now there were …
Just three speckled frogs.

Three little speckled frogs,
Sitting on a hollow log,
Eating a most delicious meal.

One jumped into the creek,
The other frogs all said EEEK!
Now there were …
Just two speckled frogs.

Two little speckled frogs,
Sitting on a hollow log,
Eating a most delicious meal.

One jumped into the creek,
The other frog didn't speak.
He was just a …
Lonely little speckled frog.

Pattern

This page may be photocopied by the purchasing institution only.

Brilliant Publications
www.brilliantpublication.co.uk

Storytelling with Puppets, Props and Playful Tales
Written by Mary Jo Huff

Story corners and playful tales

Creating a story corner

The story corner provides the storytellers and the children with a special place to enter the world of language, imagination, and creative drama. Create your story corner to fit your needs. Adapt the following ideas to suit you, your children, and the space and resources you have available. Children develop literacy skills, interact with the teacher and each other, and have fun using their imaginations.

Seating
The storyteller can stand or sit on a chair, stool, or rocking chair. The listeners may sit on a special storytelling rug, the floor, a quilt, or a story sheet.

Equipment
A well-equipped story corner should contain:

- storytelling apron
- puppet mascot
- story board
- tape recorder

- storytelling mitten or glove
- puppet stage
- magnetic board
- musical instruments

Story-starters
Story-starters help children get ready for story time.

Puppets
Puppets make stories come alive, and are one of the most powerful tools for the storyteller. Puppets should have a special place in the story corner.

Props
Props should always be available for the storyteller. Some props may announce an upcoming story. Props will increase interest in, and encourage participation in, the story.

Organizing
Include a story file in the story corner. This file should contain information for future reference.

Story rug
Children can sit on their own special story rug – a carpet remnant. Names can be added with fabric paint.

Brilliant Publications
www.brilliantpublications.co.uk

Storytelling with Puppets, Props and Playful Tales
Written by Mary Jo Huff

Story clues

Story clues posted around the room can create interest for an upcoming story. Small pictures to which you add a piece of hook fastening can be placed on a loop nylon story board or taped to poster board.

Story boxes

Children delight in decorating shoe, cereal, or other boxes with scenes from their favourite stories. Boxes can be kept in the story corner for story retelling.

Building a story wall

A portable story wall may be just what you need. By standing it at an angle from the wall, you create a storytelling area that you can set up at story time. Place area rugs or carpet remnants in the space. The wall can be moved, and can be reversed.

Construction materials for a portable wall

Measurements for portable wall:

      1.5 metre x 2 metre sheet of pegboard

      1.5 metre x 2 metre sheet of plywood

      150 mm x 50 mm x 2.5 metre board – for base

      150 mm x 50 mm x 2.5 metre board – for top

      100 mm x 50 mm x 2 metre board – for sides and centre

      100 mm x 50 mm x 2 metre board – for bottom braces

3 heavy-duty locking casters

Molding strip – to cover seam in centre

Loop nylon fabric

Corkboard or ceiling tiles

Box or wood for flower box (optional)

Cardboard or fabric for window dressing

Multi-pocket shoe holder

If you cannot obtain loop nylon fabric, you could use another typ e of fabric instead. Sew or stick strips of loop nylon tape (Velcro™) to the board. This will enable you to attach characters and props with hook fastening to the board.

Portable wall sections

Side 1:

Corkboard section. The upper left corner of the wall can be used as an announcement board. Information of any kind can be pinned there: when story time will be, who the storyteller will be, any daily information, photos of the children, drawings, and so on.

Loop nylon section. This lower area should be covered with loop nylon fabric. A seated storyteller can use it as a story board, puppets or props with hook fastening can be displayed there, announcements or art projects can be featured – it can be used in a variety of ways. Children can manipulate story characters at this level.

Puppet window. The upper right corner of the wall will contain the puppet window opening. The puppeteer may stand on either side of the opening and show the puppets through it.

Puppet storage. The lower right corner holds the puppets. A multi-pocket shoe holder will provide a home for a number of puppets.

Side 2:

Pegboard section. Pegboard is used in the upper right corner of the wall. The area can hold hooks for props or other materials.

Loop nylon section. The lower right corner should be covered with loop nylon fabric. The storyteller can sit on the floor and use the fabric area for storytelling.

Puppet window. Make the window cutout on the upper left side large enough for several puppets to be seen through it but still conceal the puppeteer. Shutters or fabric curtains are a nice added feature.

Under-window area. A small window box can be attached at the base of the window opening to display paper flowers, story props, or story clues. The area below can be covered with cork or ceiling tiles to display pinned-up items.

Brilliant Publications
www.brilliantpublications.co.uk

Storytelling with Puppets, Props and Playful Tales
Written by Mary Jo Huff

Setting up a story file

A story file will not only keep track of all the stories you have developed for storytelling; it will also remind you of the particular puppets and props that have been created and can be used with them.

To set up a story file, use a suitable box and filing cards. The following example shows the type of information you may want to include about each story in your repertoire. Alternatively, you could set up a story file database on your computer.

TITLE _____

AUTHOR _____

PUBLISHER _____ DATE _____

PROPS _____

PUPPETS _____

COMMENTS_____

Storytelling apron

Storytelling can be very exciting with the interactive storytelling apron. The storyteller actually wears the story board, and story puppets and props appear from inside the pockets.

Materials

Apron pattern
1 metre loop nylon fabric
0.5 metre cotton twill
2.3 metres soft cloth tape
Safety pin
Thread
Scissors
Sewing machine

Directions

Cut out the apron pieces according to the pattern. Sew together using a zigzag stitch with the soft, or loop, side of the nylon fabric facing out. Hem the bottom edge of the cotton twill and turn up to create the pockets (the depth of the pockets can be adjusted by cutting out a larger or smaller piece of cotton twill). Make two seams to create three pockets and overstitch to reinforce. Turn the curved areas of the apron under 2.5 cm and stitch down to create tunnels. Turn the straight edges under and stitch down. Thread the soft cloth tape through the tunnels using a large safety pin at one end to pull it through. The tape allows you to adjust the apron to fit. Puppets and props that are placed on the apron must have a piece of hook fastening on the back.

23cm

35.5cm

2.5cm hem

48cm

67cm

17cm

1cm turned hem

If you cannot obtain loop nylon fabric, make the apron from a different fabric and sew or stick strips of loop nylon tape (Velcro™) to it in suitable locations.

Using the apron

Storytelling with the apron provides children with creative, hands-on literature experiences.

Preparations

◎ Choose a story with 8 to 10 main characters and props. Having too many pieces on the apron can distract both the teller and the listeners.

◎ Create story puppets and props from laminated paper, poster board, felt, art foam, by adding a piece of hook fastening to the back. Flat puppets and props work best. Pieces that are too rounded will not hang properly.

◎ Attach a small piece of self-adhesive hook fastening to each story piece so that it will stick to the apron.

◎ Place the puppets and props in the apron pockets with the picture side facing in. This will allow you to find the character you need quickly and easily.

◎ When you're ready to tell the story, invite the children to the story corner. Tell the children the name of the book and its author, and hold up the book so they can see it.

◎ After you've finished telling the story, make the book available for the children.

Telling the story

To use the story apron, you will need to stand and face the listeners so the apron can be seen. As you speak, turn your body slightly from side to side so all the children can view the puppets and props as they're added. As a character or prop is mentioned, remove it from the pocket, turn it to face the audience, and attach it to the apron. Characters may also be attached at the beginning of a story.

Extensions

1. After the story has been told, urge the children to ask questions about the story. The children may also want to create story characters of their own to place on the apron.

2. Ask the children to create their own story with pictures. Ask them to draw 5 to 7 pictures that tell the story, or let them cut out pictures from magazines. Ask the children to tell their stories as they put the pictures in the proper sequence.

3. Stories that include colours, shapes, and numbers lend themselves to additional use of the apron for categorizing, matching and sorting.

The enormous turnip
adapted by Mary Jo Huff

Once upon a time, a local farmer went to the shop (insert the name of a shop in your community) and bought some vegetable seeds. He ploughed and tilled his garden until it was ready for planting. The farmer planted and tended the garden.

When it was time for the farmer to harvest his vegetables, he took a bucket to the garden and began pulling the vegetables out of the ground. The farmer took hold of the top of one **turnip** and began to pull. He pulled and he pulled and he pulled, but that old stubborn **turnip** would not come out of the ground.

The farmer called to his wife to come and help him. The wife took hold of the farmer and the farmer took hold of the **turnip** and they pulled and they pulled and they pulled. But that old stubborn **turnip** would not come out of the ground.

The wife called to her daughter to come and help. The daughter took hold of the wife, the wife took hold of the farmer, the farmer took hold of the **turnip**, and all together they pulled and they pulled and they pulled. But that old stubborn **turnip** would not come out of the ground.

The daughter whistled for the dog and the dog came to help. The dog took hold of the daughter, the daughter took hold of the wife, the wife took hold of the farmer, the farmer took hold of the **turnip**, and all together they pulled and they pulled and they pulled. But that old stubborn **turnip** would not come out of the ground.

The dog called to the cat to come and help. The cat took hold of the dog, the dog took hold of the daughter, the daughter took hold of the wife, the wife took hold of the farmer, the farmer took hold of the **turnip**, and all together they pulled and they pulled and they pulled. But that old stubborn **turnip** would not come out of the ground.

The cat called to the mouse to come and help. The mouse took hold of the cat, the cat took hold of the dog, the dog took hold of the daughter, the daughter took hold of the wife, the wife took hold of the farmer, the farmer took hold of the **turnip**, and all together they pulled and they pulled and they pulled. And that old stubborn **turnip** finally came out of the ground!

'Remember,' said the little mouse, 'you're never too small to help.'

(As you tell this story with the apron, place the figures so they hold on to each other. You can use a different vegetable in your story instead of a turnip.)

Story retelling
When the children retell the story, let several of them act it out, placing their hands on each other's shoulders until the **mouse** takes hold and they all fall down.

Patterns

Turnip

Farmer's wife

Farmer

This page may be photocopied by the purchasing institution only.

Brilliant Publications
www.brilliantpublications.co.uk

Storytelling with Puppets, Props and Playful Tales
Written by Mary Jo Huff

Dog

Mouse

Cat

Daughter

This page may be photocopied by the purchasing institution only.

Portable story board

This loop nylon story board can be used with a variety of tales. It can be held or set up on an easel and sized to fit your needs.

Materials
Medium-density fibreboard (MDF) or plywood cut to the desired size; loop nylon fabric; scissors, heavy flannel fabric; sewing machine; needle and thread; wood for framing (optional).

Directions
Cut a piece of loop nylon fabric and a piece of flannel about 1.5 cm larger than the MDF; measure carefully so the fabric will fit tightly around the board. With right sides together (the soft side of the loop nylon fabric), stitch up three sides, leaving a short side open. Turn right side out. Insert the board and close the open end with hand stitching. Cut and add a frame if desired.

If you cannot obtain loop nylon fabric, use flannel for both sides and stick or sew strips of loop nylon tape (Velcro™) to one side.

Story retelling
The children will enjoy using these boards to retell old and new favourite tales. Stories that work well with story tins will also work with story boards.

Five little fishes

This tale needs only five fish and a whale for telling the story on a story board. The tale can also be told on a story glove, mitten, or apron, or, by adding a magnet to each character, on a story tin.

Materials
Paper
Markers
Hook fastening
Llarge empty tin can
Scissors
Large paper plate
Glue
1 split pin fastener
Paint (ocean blue and other colours)
Brush

Directions
Fish
Cut out five fish shapes and colour as desired. Give each fish a different eye colour or shape. Glue a piece of hook fastening to the back of each fish.

Whale
Cut the paper plate in half. Cut out a tail shape and a mouth from one of the halves. Colour as desired. Glue the tail to the other half plate and attach the mouth with the split pin fastener. Glue a piece of hook fastening to the back of the whale.

Tin
Paint the can an ocean blue. Add drawings of fish, seaweed, and other ocean elements, if desired.

Story retelling
The characters can be stored in the tin and the story retold using the story board. The children will want to retell this simple counting tale again and again.

Five little fishes

Five little fishes heading for shore,
Along came a WHALE (gulp)
And then there were FOUR.

Four little fishes swimming in the sea,
Along came a WHALE (gulp)
And then there were THREE.

Three little fishes hiding from you,
Along came a WHALE (gulp)
And then there were TWO.

Two little fishes having some fun,
Along came a WHALE (gulp)
And then there was ONE.

One little fish swimming in the sun,
Along came a WHALE (gulp)
And then there was NONE.

Brilliant Publications
www.brilliantpublications.co.uk

Storytelling with Puppets, Props and Playful Tales
Written by Mary Jo Huff

Patterns

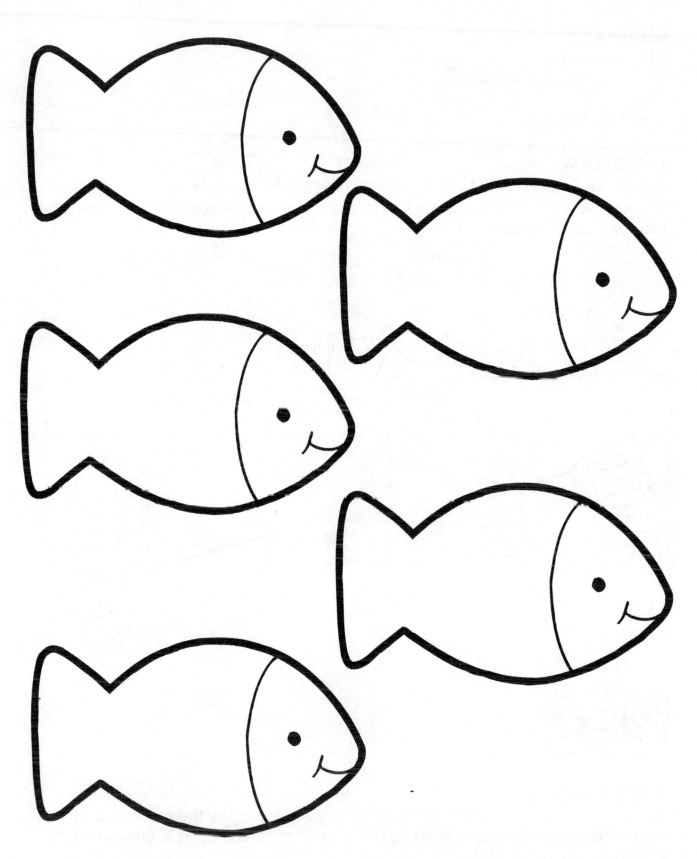

This page may be photocopied by the purchasing institution only.

Whale puppet

This whale puppet can gobble up the fish. His mouth opens very wide.

Materials

Large paper plate
Crayons, markers, or paint
Glue
1 split pin fastener

Directions

Cut the paper plate in half. Cut a section of leftover plate for the tail and glue to paper plate half. Cut another section for the mouth and attach it with the split pin fastener for movement.

Story retelling

Store the whales and fishes in a large tin that is painted like the ocean. Attach a magnet and Velcro hook to each fish and the story can be used in different story areas.

Brilliant Publications
www.brilliantpublications.co.uk

Storytelling with Puppets, Props and Playful Tales
Written by Mary Jo Huff

Storytelling waistcoat

Like the storytelling apron, the storytelling waistcoat is worn during retelling, adding another fun dimension to story time.

Materials
1 metre loop nylon fabric
4 metres colourful binding
Scissors
Thread
Sewing machine

Directions
Simple waistcoat – Make a pattern as shown below out of paper. Staple it together and try it on to check that it fits. When you are happy with your pattern, cut the waistcoat out of the loop nylon fabric. One metre of material will make a waistoat that will fit most adults. Place the sides together so the soft side is facing out and stitch across the top and down the straight sides. Oversew the edges or sew on a colourful binding.

As you tell and retell the story, attach the characters to the waistcoat as they enter the tale. Press the hook fastening on the back of the characters into the front of the waistcoat.

Storytelling aids

These storytelling props let the children be part of the story.

Mitten and glove

Materials
0.5 metre loop nylon fabric for each mitten or glove
Fabric glue or thread
Sewing machine
Scissors

Directions
Following the pattern, cut material to the size you need. Place the wrong sides together and stitch or glue.

Story retelling
Children can wear the glove or mitten and attach story characters to them during retelling. Characters must be backed with a piece of hook fastening to stick to the storytelling accessories. Stories with only two or three characters work best with these small surfaces. Gloves and mittens can also be placed in story boxes.

Patterns

Mitten

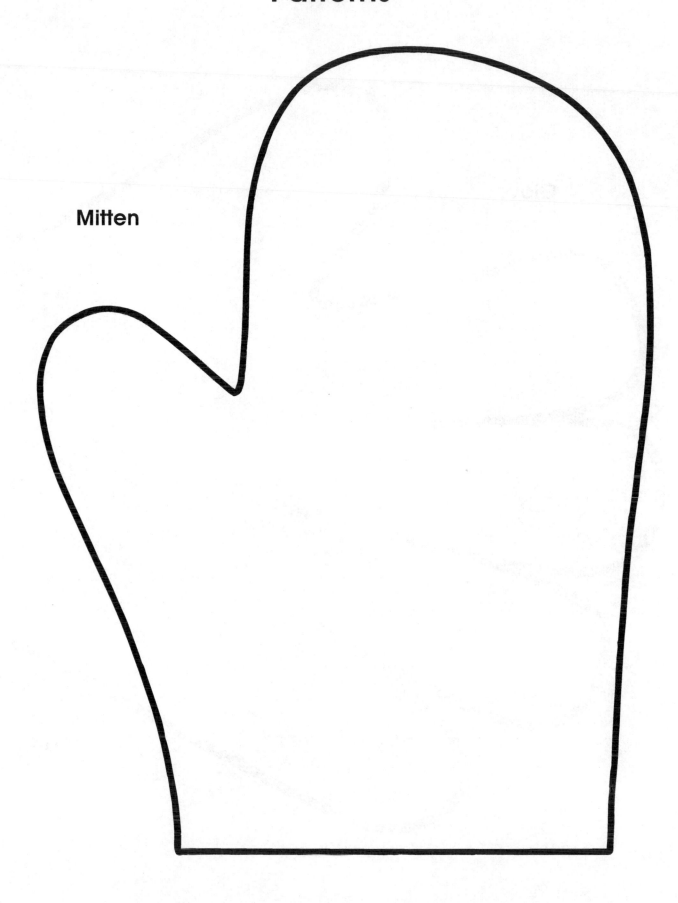

This page may be photocopied by the purchasing institution only.

Storytelling with Puppets, Props and Playful Tales
Written by Mary Jo Huff

Brilliant Publications
www.brilliantpublications.co.uk

117

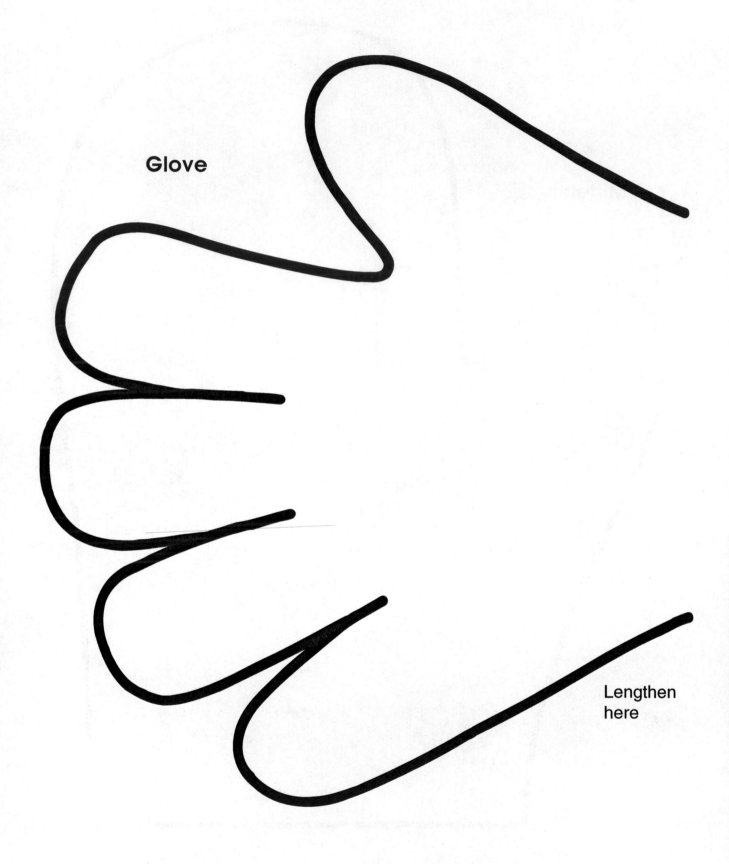

Glove

Lengthen
here

This page may be photocopied by the purchasing institution only.

Brilliant Publications
www.brilliantpublications.co.uk

Storytelling with Puppets, Props and Playful Tales
Written by Mary Jo Huff

Headband

Materials
0.5 metre loop nylon fabric cut into 5 cm wide strips
Hook fastening
Scissors

Directions
Cut a strip of loop nylon fabric to size. Attach a piece of hook fastening to the end on the inside of the fabric. This allows the headband to be adjusted to any size.

Story retelling
The children can become part of the story they are retelling by attaching characters with hook fastening on the back to their headbands. Remind the children to attach only small characters and to place them so their sight is not blocked. Headbands can be stored by clipping them to string clotheslines strung across the story corner.

5 cm

Storytelling box

Story characters can be stored on the inside and stories can be told on the outside of this story box. Before you begin a story, ask the children what they think is inside the box.

Materials
Cardboard box with lid (a copier paper box works well)
Loop nylon fabric and hook fastening
Glue
Scissors
Stapler
Paint and brush (optional)

Directions
Cut the fabric to fit the box and glue it on with the soft side out. Staple the edges. Paint the lid or cover it with fabric. Attach a small piece of hook fastening to the characters you will use to tell the story. The box can be designed to work with themes, such as festivals, seasons, farm animals, or fairy tales, and for special festivals, such as Valentine's Day, Guy Fawkes' Night, or Christmas.

Story retelling
Place story characters, books, and props such as magic wands and headbands inside the box. Keep the box in the story corner and let children delight in retelling stories using the box's surface.

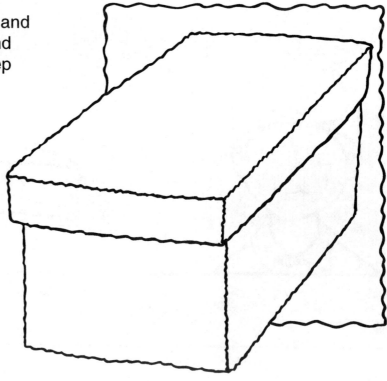

Storytelling with Puppets, Props and Playful Tales
Written by Mary Jo Huff

Storytelling cube

A soft three-dimensional cube invites children to sit down with it to retell a good story.

Materials

1 metre loop nylon fabric
Scissors
Needle and thread
Sewing machine
Quilt stuffing/padding

Directions

Cut out six squares of material exactly the same size. Sew the pieces together with wrong sides facing together, leaving one seam open for stuffing. Turn inside out so the soft side is facing out. Stuff the cube firmly with quilt padding and sew closed the last seam.

Story retelling

The children can use this cube by rotating it and placing characters on the sides, top, and bottom. Stories that can be retold well with a cube include: **The Little Red Hen**, **The Three Little Pigs**, **Brown Bear, Brown Bear, What Do You See?** by Bill Martin, and **I Went Walking** by Sue Williams.

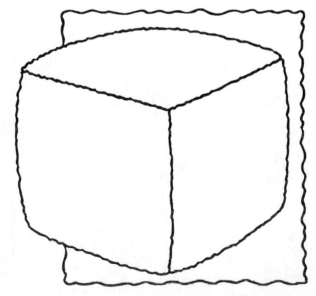

Storytelling tin can

Use the story tin as a story centre in which the children keep pictures that illustrate stories they've made up or like to retell.

Materials

A large empty tin can (eg for formula milk)
Spray paint
Laminator
Scissors
Old magazines
Paper
Markers or crayons

Directions

Spray paint the tin can. Let the children find pictures or draw pictures that illustrate a favourite story. Laminate the pictures and place them in the tin.

Story retelling

Keep the can in the story corner. Let the children reach into the can and share a story through their pictures.

Storytelling bag

Before you start telling a story, let the children reach into this bag and try to guess what the story will be about.

Materials
White pillowcase
Fabric crayons
Fabric paint
Iron
Ponytail scrunchy

Directions
Choose a story and use the fabric crayons and paint to draw on the pillowcase a design that illustrates the tale. Place items in the bag that will be visual aids for telling the story. Keep the bag closed with a ponytail scrunchy. A baby pillowcase can be used for young children or for stories with very few props.

Story retelling
Put the story bag in the story corner for children to use in tale retelling. Keeping the story aids in the bag creates a sense of excitement and wonder.

Storytelling helpers

Storytellers often need help in getting ready to tell their stories, and in placing figures and props on storytelling surfaces. Children will love taking it in turns being the story helper, and you can make choosing helpers fair by using name tins to keep track of who has helped you.

Materials

2 large empty tins (eg for formula milk)
Spray paint
Vinyl letters
Laminated paper
Permanent marker

Directions

Spray-paint each tin a different colour. Use the vinyl letters to label one tin 'Storytelling Helpers 1' and the other tin 'Story Helpers 2'. Print each child's name on a piece of heavy laminated paper and put all the papers in can 1. Each time you need a storytelling helper, draw a name from tin 1 and then place it in tin 2. When all the names have been chosen, start choosing names from tin 2 and store them in tin 1. The children will soon understand the process and figure out which tin holds their name. If you like, let each child add a special sticker to his or her name card.

Brilliant Publications
www.brilliantpublications.co.uk

Storytelling with Puppets, Props and Playful Tales
Written by Mary Jo Huff

Puppet stage

A portable puppet stage provides a special place for the children to tell stories and pretend with their puppets. While stages can be constructed, three-panelled cardboard display units make excellent stages and are easy to obtain from most craft or school supply shops. One unit can be used in the story corner or children can create individual stages to use on their own.

To use the display unit as a puppet stage, cut out a good-sized opening from the middle panel for the puppet to be seen through. Then decorate to suit a particular story, for example:

◎ sponge-paint a wild animal or farm animal scene
◎ stamp the child's hand print and add the child's name for use with a variety of stories
◎ paint on a flower garden
◎ use markers to make a space scene
◎ use watercolours for an ocean scene
◎ use crayons to create a circus
◎ glue on collage items.

Set the three-sided unit on a table top when you are about to tell a puppet story, and fold for easy storage.

Puppet stage ideas

This page may be photocopied by the purchasing institution only.

Brilliant Publications
www.brilliantpublications.co.uk

Storytelling with Puppets, Props and Playful Tales
Written by Mary Jo Huff

Resources

Story books for storytelling

Allen, Pamela, **Who Sank the Boat?** (Puffin 2000).
Brett, Jan, **The Mitten** (Hodder Wayland, 1999).
Carle, Eric, **The Very Hungry Caterpillar** (Puffin Books, 1974).
Eastman, P.D., **Are You My Mother?** (Harper Collins, 1982).
Fox, Mem, **Possum Magic** (Harsourt Paperback,1991).
Fox, Mem, **Wilfred Gordon McDonald Partridge** (Puffin Books,1987).
Gray, Libba Moore, **Miss Tizzy** (Aladdin Paperbacks, 1998).
Hutchins, Pat, **Rosie's Walk** (Puffin Books,1970).
Lionni, Leo, **Little Blue and Little Yellow, A story for Pippo and
    other children** (Mulberry Books, 1995).
MacDonald, Amy, **Little Beaver and the Echo** (Walker Books, 1993).
Martin, Bill, **Brown Bear, Brown Bear, What Do You See?**, (Puffin Books,
    1995).
Shaw, Charles, **It Looked Like Spilt Milk** (Harper Collins Publishers, 1988).
Stevens, Janet, **Tops and Bottoms** (Hazar Publishing, 1997).
Williams, Sue, **I Went Walking** (Voyager Books, 1992).

Story telling aids

Books

Baltuck, Naomi and Cushman, Doug, **Crazy Gibberish and Other Story Hour Stretches** (Linnet Books, 1993).

Grugeon, Elizabeth and Gordin, Paul, **The Art of Storytelling for Teachers and Pupils** (David Fulton, 2000)

Kinghorn, Harriet and Pelton, Mary Helen, **Every Child a Storyteller** (Libraries Unlimited, 1991).

MacDonald, Margaret Read, **The Storyteller's Start-up Book** (August House, 1993).

Melton, Nancy, **The Art of Storytelling** (Element Books, 1998).

Raines, Shirley and Canady, Robert, **Story Stretchers** (Gryphon, 1989).

Van Schuyver, Jan and Hester, Ellen Kae, **Storytelling Made Easy with Puppets** (Oryx, 1993).

Materials

Loop nylon fabric is the generic name for Velcro™. It is available by the metre, along with various hook and loop fastening products and staples, glue and so on, from:

> Fibrous Ltd
> Unit 11, Parker International Estate
> Platt St, off Astley St
> Dukinfield, Cheshire SK16 4QZ
> Tel: 0161 343 6008

Various supplies for story corners, puppets and props are available from:

> Hope Educational Ltd
> Orb Mill
> Huddersfield Rd
> Oldham, Lancashire OL4 2ST
> Tel: 0161 633 6611

Printed in the United Kingdom
by Lightning Source UK Ltd.
99802UKS00001B/1-102